Albert Einstein

by Anita Yasuda

MEDIA ENHANCED BOOKS
AV2 BY WEIGL
ADDED VALUE • AUDIO VISUAL

www.av2books.com

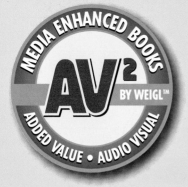

AV² BY WEIGL™
MEDIA ENHANCED BOOKS
ADDED VALUE • AUDIO VISUAL

Go to **www.av2books.com,** and enter this book's unique code.

BOOK CODE

J709360

AV² by **Weigl** brings you media enhanced books that support active learning.

AV² provides enriched content that supplements and complements this book. Weigl's AV² books strive to create inspired learning and engage young minds in a total learning experience.

Your AV² Media Enhanced books come alive with...

 Audio
Listen to sections of the book read aloud.

 Key Words
Study vocabulary, and complete a matching word activity.

 Video
Watch informative video clips.

 Quizzes
Test your knowledge.

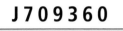 **Embedded Weblinks**
Gain additional information for research.

 Slide Show
View images and captions, and prepare a presentation.

 Try This!
Complete activities and hands-on experiments.

... and much, much more!

Published by AV² by Weigl
350 5th Avenue, 59th Floor
New York, NY 10118

www.av2books.com   www.weigl.com

Library of Congress Cataloging-in-Publication Data

Yasuda, Anita.
 Albert Einstein / Anita Yasuda.
     p. cm. — (Icons)
Includes index.
ISBN 978-1-62127-305-9 (hardcover : alk. paper) —
ISBN 978-1-62127-311-0 (softcover : alk. paper)
1. Einstein, Albert, 1879-1955—Juvenile literature.
2. Physicists—Biography—Juvenile literature. I. Title.
QC16.E5Y376 2014
530.092—dc23
[B]
                        2013000834

Printed in the United States of America in Brainerd, Minnesota
3 4 5 6 7 8 9 0 20 19 18 17 16

250216
022016

Editor: Megan Cuthbert
Design: Tammy West

Photograph Credits
Weigl acknowledges Getty Images as the primary image supplier for this title. Every reasonable effort has been made to trace ownership and to obtain permission to reprint copyright material. The publishers would be pleased to have any errors or omissions brought to their attention so that they may be corrected in subsequent printings.

Contents

Who Was Albert Einstein?

Albert Einstein is one of the most respected scientists of the 20th century. His exciting ideas, or **theories,** not only changed **physics**, but the way people saw the world. Albert's theories on light, space, and time have led to many inventions, from cell phones to Global Positioning Systems (GPS). Albert Einstein's ideas continue to influence the world.

Albert is best known for a series of scientific papers he wrote in 1905. One of these papers is known as the **Theory of Relativity**. After Albert's theory was proven to be correct in 1919, he became an international celebrity. Albert used his celebrity to promote peace and to voice his concerns about the impact of science on nature.

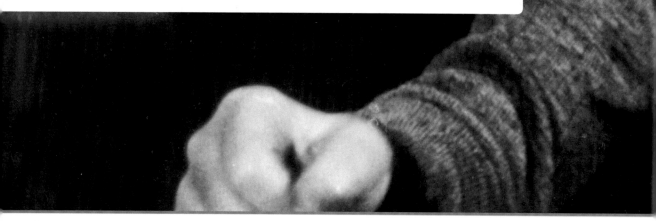

"*Anyone who has never made a mistake has never tried anything new.*"

Growing Up

Albert Einstein was born on March 14, 1879 in Ulm, Germany. The Einstein family moved to Munich a few weeks later. Albert's parents, Hermann and Pauline, hoped Munich would be good for the family's electrical manufacturing business. In 1881, Albert's sister Maria, nicknamed Maja, was born.

The Einsteins were a close-knit Jewish family. Their home was always filled with music. Albert's mother, Pauline, was a talented pianist. Albert was musical, too. He started playing violin at the age of six. Albert studied musical pieces by classical composers. Besides music, Albert loved puzzles and building houses out of cards. He could often be found lying on the family sofa doing mathematical problems.

◀ In Munich, Germany, Hermann Einstein and his brother founded Elektrotechnische Fabrik J. Einstein & Cie, a company that manufactured electrical equipment.

Get to Know Germany

NETHERLANDS

GERMANY

BELGIUM

POLAND

CZECH REPUBLIC

N

SCALE
0   50 Miles

0   50 Kilometers

Germany has a population of more than 80 million people. It is the second most populated country in Europe.

The tallest church in the world is located in Ulm, Germany. The Ulm Münster is 528 feet (161 meters) tall.

Berlin is Germany's capital city and also one of the country's 16 states. It is the largest city in Germany, with a population of 3.5 million.

Germany is known for creating more than 300 types of bread and more than 1,500 kinds of sausage.

STATE SYMBOLS

TREE
Oak

BIRD
Eagle

FLOWER
Cornflower

Practice Makes Perfect

In high school, Albert earned top marks in Latin, physics, geometry, and mathematics, but he found the school system in Munich too strict. Albert liked to ask questions in class. His seventh grade teacher became tired of Albert's questions. He found Albert to be disrespectful. He predicted that Albert would never get very far in life.

At home, Albert read as many books as he could. This included science, mathematics, and history books. Instead of playing with friends, Albert preferred to read textbooks. If Albert did not understand something, he spent hours on the problem until he solved it.

When Albert was 15, his family moved to Milan, Italy. Albert stayed behind in a Munich boarding school. He later quit school and joined his family in Italy. His family was very worried that he had not graduated from high school.

◀ Einstein completed high school in Aarau, Switzerland. He graduated with the highest grades in his class.

In Switzerland, there was a **polytechnic** school that would accept students without a high school diploma. Students could enroll as long as they passed the school's entrance exam. At 16, Albert left for Switzerland to take the entrance test. He easily passed the math and physics portions. He did not do as well on the other sections. On the advice of the principal of the school, Albert attended a nearby public school in the town of Aarau. Here, Albert was able to fill the gaps in his education. He loved his new school. A year later, in 1896, Albert enrolled at the Federal Polytechnic in Zurich. He began studying for a teaching diploma in mathematics and physics. He was on his way to becoming a scientist.

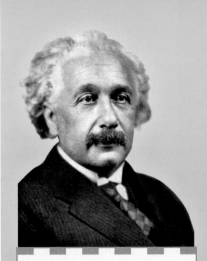

QUICK FACTS

- The Einstein crater on the Moon is named after Albert Einstein.

- Albert liked to visualize problems in his mind instead of performing experiments in a lab. He called these 'thought experiments.'

- Albert published more than 300 scientific papers during his lifetime.

◄ While living in Zurich, Albert decided to give up his German citizenship. He became a Swiss citizen in 1901.

Key Events

Albert continued to study, and in 1905, he completed his **thesis**. At the age of 26, Albert was awarded his doctoral degree by the University of Zurich. That same year, he published four of his most important scientific papers in a physics journal. The year 1905 is often called Albert's 'Miracle Year.' His papers on light, time, and space contained groundbreaking ideas.

In his relativity paper, Albert suggested that the Sun's gravity could bend light. This could only be observed during a solar eclipse. In 1919, British astronomer Sir Arthur Eddington confirmed Albert's theory. This confirmation made Albert Einstein's name known throughout the world.

Albert's second paper proved there were **atoms** and **molecules**. The third paper explained his theory on time and space. It suggested why scientists had problems measuring the speed of light. The fourth paper showed the relationship between energy and **mass**. He completed his Theory of Relativity in 1916.

◀ **After slowly gaining academic recognition for his theories, Albert was invited to lecture and discuss his ideas at international meetings.**

Thoughts from Albert

Albert used his fame to promote world peace and to work for the public good. Here are some of the comments he made about himself, the world, and peace.

Albert talks about how he sees the world.
"The eternal mystery of the world is its comprehensibility...The fact that it is comprehensible is a miracle."

Albert talks about peace.
"Peace cannot be kept by force. It can only be achieved by understanding."

Albert talks about the importance of being an individual.
"It is important to foster individuality, for only the individual can produce the new ideas."

Albert talks about the importance of trying your hardest even if a goal seems out of reach.
"One should not pursue goals that are easily achieved. One must develop an instinct for what one can just barely achieve through one's greatest efforts."

Albert talks about how he sees himself.
"I have no special talents. I am only passionately curious."

Albert talks about the importance of taking action.
"The world is a dangerous place, not because of those who do evil, but because of those who look on and do nothing."

What Is a Scientist?

Scientists are creative, curious, and want to learn new things. Albert Einstein never stopped asking questions. Scientists like to solve problems. They will often develop an idea, or hypothesis, to answer a problem. In order to prove their hypothesis correct, they will research and conduct experiments. This process can take a very long time. Scientists gain knowledge and information from their experiments. Even when a hypothesis is proven to be wrong, scientists can still learn new information from their mistakes. Some scientists, such as Albert, achieve international recognition for their work.

There are many different types of science. In high school, students who wish to study science might study physics, chemistry, biology, and mathematics. In university, there are even more science subjects. Scientists have a wide range of careers to choose from. Scientists must be dedicated as they work very long hours.

▶ Albert often met with fellow scientists, including fellow Nobel Prize winner Irène Joilot Curie, who won the prize for her work in chemistry.

THEORY

Theories are used to try to understand and explain the world around us. In the scientific world, a theory is a group of ideas that are confirmed through extensive testing, observation, and experiments. These theories can then be used to gain further scientific knowledge. Theories often change and develop as scientists learn more information.

Scientists 101

Benjamin Franklin (1706–1790)

Benjamin was a scientist, inventor, and a statesman. He was born on January 17, 1706. His inventions include the bifocal lens and the odometer. In the early 1750s, he used a kite to prove that lightning was electricity. Ben developed the lightning rod to protect people and buildings from lightning. The rod attracts lightning and sends the charge into the ground. That way, the lightning will not cause harm.

Thomas Edison (1847–1931)

Thomas was born on February 11, 1847. Thomas was taught at home by his mother after a schoolteacher commented that he was slow. Thomas enjoyed learning about how mechanical things worked. He also liked experimenting with chemicals. He worked in a variety of jobs but became best known for his inventions. Among his most notable inventions are the light bulb, a motion picture camera, and a phonograph. In total, Thomas **patented** 1,093 of his inventions.

George Washington Carver (1864–1943)

George was born into slavery around 1864. After slavery was abolished, George was one of the first African American students to study at college. George gained a reputation as a brilliant **botanist**. He was able to show that the peanut could be made into more than 300 products. By the 1930s, peanuts were a million dollar industry. George received many awards, including a Roosevelt Medal for his contributions to Southern agriculture.

Barbara McClintock (1902–1992)

Barbara McClintock was born on June 16, 1902, in Hartford, Connecticut. She studied at Cornell University and became interested in the study of **genetics**. Barbara became known for her work on how genes in crops of maize could change position. Her discovery that genes could move around earned her the Nobel Prize in Physiology or Medicine in 1983. Barbara earned many other awards, including the National Medal of Science.

Influences

The Einsteins recognized their young son's fascination with the natural world. They encouraged his interest in math and science and often gave him science books. When Albert was only five years old, his father gave him a toy magnetic compass. The gift fascinated Albert for hours. Albert wanted to know what invisible force was making the needle point north.

Albert did not have to wonder alone. Scientific and technological conversations were a part of daily life in Albert's home. Albert's father and his Uncle Jakob were electrical engineers. The family's electrical business used advanced technology for the time.

Uncle Jakob took a special interest in Albert's education. He enjoyed explaining geometry and **algebra** to Albert. Jakob challenged Albert with difficult problems and made math into a game. Albert would work on math problems for days.

◀ Albert's early love of math and physics led him to seek a career as a teacher. He had two temporary positions as a mathematics teacher.

Albert's skill in mathematics amazed his Uncle Jakob and another frequent visitor to the Einstein home, Max Talmud. Max was a poor Polish medical student who was given free meals by the Einsteins. Max brought science and geometry books for Albert. He treated Albert as an equal and talked with him for hours about science, math, and **philosophy**.

THE EINSTEIN FAMILY

The Einstein home was loving and supportive. Hermann and Pauline encouraged Albert in his studies. Albert remained close to his sister, Maja, his entire life. In 1903, Albert married his first wife, Mileva Maric. They had two sons, Hans Albert and Eduard. The couple divorced in 1919. Albert married his second wife, Elsa, in 1919. After Elsa died in 1936, Maja moved into Albert's Princeton, New Jersey home.

▶ Albert's sister, Maja, was born two years after Albert. She became Albert's closest childhood friend.

Overcoming Obstacles

When Albert graduated from the Swiss Polytechnic, he had difficulty finding a job. He wrote to many professors asking for a position as an assistant, but no one gave him a job. Albert found a little work tutoring students in mathematics and physics, but this did not pay much.

Two years later, Albert was offered a permanent position in the Swiss Patent Office in Bern. This was his first steady job. However, Albert remained committed to science. Now that Albert had a fulltime job, he could stop worrying about money and instead work on his own theories. He found time to write after work. This dedication allowed Albert to produce his scientific papers. He formed a club called The Olympia Academy with two other students. They would meet to discuss science and philosophy. These meetings provided Albert with the chance to explain his theories on physics.

◀ **Albert evaluated patent applications at the Swiss Patent Office. It was well-paid and undemanding work that allowed him the freedom to concentrate on his scientific studies.**

▲ Scientists who worked on the Manhattan Project had to maintain complete secrecy. Albert was never directly involved in the program or the creation of atomic weapons.

Following the success of his scientific papers, Albert toured the world giving lectures about his theories. During this time, there was unrest in Europe. Albert did not like the changes taking place in Europe. He moved to the United States in 1933.

Just before World War II began, Albert wrote to the president of the United States, Franklin D. Roosevelt. Albert told Roosevelt that he thought Germany was developing an **atomic weapon**. President Roosevelt was impressed by the letter and began the Manhattan Project. The aim of the top-secret project was to create an atomic bomb. After the war, Albert devoted his life to making people understand the dangers of atomic weapons.

Achievements and Successes

Albert's scientific breakthroughs changed science. Albert was able to show that light was made of tiny invisible particles, now called photons. Before 1905, people did not know this. They believed light only moved in waves. Light is both a particle and a wave. In 1921, Albert received the highest prize in science for this discovery, the Nobel Prize in Physics.

Throughout his life, Albert received awards and honorary degrees from schools around the world. Albert received one such award, the Copley Medal, in 1925. Ten years later, Albert received the Franklin Medal from the Franklin Institute. This award paid tribute to his contributions in theoretical physics.

▲ **The National Academy of Science in Washington D.C. honored Albert with a monument in 1979. The academy unveiled the monument on the 100th anniversary of Albert's birth.**

Albert continued his research and devoted his life to many **humanitarian** causes. Though offered the presidency of Israel in 1952, Albert turned it down. Three years later, Albert died.

In 2005, the United Nations marked the 100th anniversary of Albert's 'Miracle Year'. They declared it to be 'The World Year of Physics.' Scientists from around the world met to discuss Albert's work. Events were held on almost every continent.

HELPING OTHERS

During his lifetime, Albert Einstein supported many charities and organizations that promoted peace. Albert co-founded The Emergency Committee of Atomic Scientists in 1946 to warn the public about the dangers of atomic weapons.

During World War II, Albert Einstein handwrote his Theory of Relativity and auctioned it off to support the war effort. The paper raised six million dollars. At Albert's suggestion, the International Rescue Committee was founded in 1933. The organization continues to help support people fleeing from war.

Albert was able to leave Europe before World War II and was dedicated to helping other refugees. He did not believe in war and spoke out against it publicly.

Write a Biography

A person's life story can be the subject of a book. This kind of book is called a biography. Biographies describe the lives of remarkable people, such as those who have achieved great success or have done important things to help others. These people may be alive today, or they may have lived many years ago. Reading a biography can help you learn more about a remarkable person.

At school, you might be asked to write a biography. First, decide who you want to write about. You can choose a scientist, such as Albert Einstein, or any other person. Then, find out if your library has any books about this person. Learn as much as you can about him or her. Write down the key events in this person's life. What was this person's childhood like? What has he or she accomplished? What are his or her goals? What makes this person special or unusual?

A concept web is a useful research tool. Read the questions in the following concept web. Answer the questions in your notebook. Your answers will help you write a biography.

Writing a Biography

Adulthood

- Where does this individual currently reside?
- Does he or she have a family?

Your Opinion

- What did you learn from the books you read in your research?
- Would you suggest these books to others?
- Was anything missing from these books?

Childhood

- Where and when was this person born?
- Describe his or her parents, siblings, and friends.
- Did this person grow up in unusual circumstances?

Main Accomplishments

- What is this person's life's work?
- Has he or she received awards or recognition for accomplishments?
- How have this person's accomplishments served others?

Work and Preparation

- What was this person's education?
- What was his or her work experience?
- How does this person work; what is or was the process he or she uses or used?

Help and Obstacles

- Did this individual have a positive attitude?
- Did he or she receive help from others?
- Did this person have a mentor?
- Did this person face any hardships?
- If so, how were the hardships overcome?

Timeline

YEAR	ALBERT EINSTEIN	WORLD EVENTS
1879	Albert Einstein is born.	Joseph Swan demonstrates the world's first working electrical light bulb using carbon filament.
1900	Albert graduates with a degree in physics from the Swiss Federal Polytechnic School in Zurich.	The first affordable hand-held camera, called the 'Brownie', is produced by Kodak in the United States.
1905	Albert publishes four breakthrough scientific papers and his thesis in his 'Miracle Year'.	The Wright brothers' plane, *The Flyer III*, becomes the first plane able to fly for long periods of time.
1916	Albert completes his General Theory of Relativity.	Germany declares war against Portugal.
1921	Albert is awarded a Nobel Prize for his work in physics.	Adolf Hitler becomes Chairman of the Nazi Party of Germany.
1939	Einstein recommends to President Roosevelt that the United States begin atomic research.	World War II begins after Nazi Germany attacks Poland.
1955	Albert dies at the age of 76 on April 18 in Princeton, New Jersey.	The Russell-Einstein **manifesto** is released. Written by prominent scientists, it urges countries not to use atomic weapons.

Key Words

algebra: a branch of mathematics used to find an unknown quantity

atomic weapon: a device, such as a bomb or warhead, that can cause mass destruction

atoms: tiny particles

botanist: a scientist who studies plants

genetics: the science that deals with how characteristics are passed from parents to their children

humanitarian: helping people in need

manifesto: a publicly released statement that declares the intentions or opinions of the writers

mass: the quantity of matter that a body contains

molecules: groups of atoms bonded together

patented: obtained a government document that gives inventors the rights to an invention, so they are the only one who can create and sell it

philosophy: the study of reality, knowledge, and life

physics: the study of energy, matter, and forces in the world

polytechnic: a school that specializes in applied sciences and industrial arts

theories: ideas that try to explain a group of facts

Theory of Relativity: two theories that discuss the speed of light and how gravity works

thesis: a formal piece of writing written by a university student for an advanced degree

Index

Log on to www.av2books.com

AV² by Weigl brings you media enhanced books that support active learning. Go to www.av2books.com, and enter the special code found on page 2 of this book. You will gain access to enriched and enhanced content that supplements and complements this book. Content includes video, audio, weblinks, quizzes, a slide show, and activities.

AV² Online Navigation

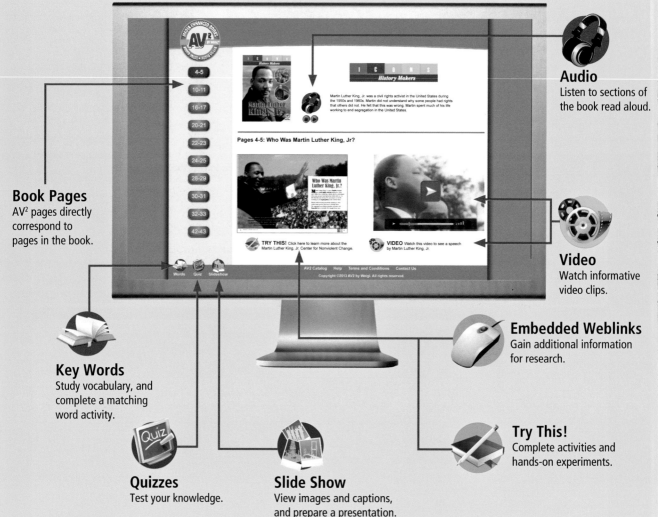

Audio
Listen to sections of the book read aloud.

Book Pages
AV² pages directly correspond to pages in the book.

Video
Watch informative video clips.

Embedded Weblinks
Gain additional information for research.

Key Words
Study vocabulary, and complete a matching word activity.

Try This!
Complete activities and hands-on experiments.

Quizzes
Test your knowledge.

Slide Show
View images and captions, and prepare a presentation.

AV² was built to bridge the gap between print and digital. We encourage you to tell us what you like and what you want to see in the future.

Sign up to be an AV² Ambassador at www.av2books.com/ambassador.